Where Is Suzie's Tooth

By Sonya Connor

To Dylan
Love,
Grandpa Steve
April 8, 2023

Where is Suzie's Tooth

This is a work of fiction. Names, characters, places, and incidents either are the product of the author's imagination or are used fictitiously. Any resemblance to actual persons, living or dead, events, or locales is entirely coincidental.

Copyright © 2022 by Sonya Connor

All rights reserved. No part of this book may be reproduced or used in any manner without written permission of the copyright owner except for the use of quotations in a book review. For more information: sunshinereadingadventures.com.

First paperback edition October 2022

ISBN 978-0-9991385-3-3 (paperback)
Library of Congress Control Number: 2022916993

www.sunshinereadingadventures.com

Suzie smiles and sees a row of teeth.
A row of teeth that help her eat.
But when she brushes her teeth today.
One was wobbly with a little sway.

A little rocky it seems to be.
Maybe she should just let it be.
She flosses her teeth in-between.
Brush and floss to keep them clean.

Leave it alone and carry on.
There is no need for concern.
Suzie sees that it's time to scoot.
No time to worry about her tooth.

Suzie has an apple with her lunch.
She takes a bite, a very large crunch.
Her tooth pops out onto her plate.
Her tooth came out as she ate.

She saves her tooth to take it home.
It left a space shaped as a dome.
She points to show her mom the spot.
Her tooth was there, but now it's not.

Suzie soon forgets about her tooth.
Busy days in the life of this youth.
Then one day another tooth pops out.
It goes flying out of her mouth.

The arch in her mouth is now larger.
Clearly visible when she smiles wider.
A sign of growing up, baby teeth gone.
Suzie shows proudly with a big yawn.

Suzie now chews with her side teeth.
Taking in smaller bites to eat.
Another girl in class flashes a smile.
She's been missing two teeth for a while.

Suzie needs her teeth to eat and smile.
It is okay if they are gone for a while.
New teeth will grow in the place.
To soon fill in the arch shaped space.

One day Suzie looks at her mouth.
New teeth are beginning to sprout.
In her gums tiny specks of white.
Soon to be used to take a bite.

Two teeth are growing side by side.
One tooth, two teeth, smile so wide.
Halfway grown they seem strong now.
Front teeth crunch they will allow.

Another day Suzie looks again.
She sees the gap is now filled in.
Her row of teeth is now complete.
With two new teeth to use to eat.

Her friend too shows off new chompers.
Replacements for those toothy poppers.
Along the top of the teeth are ridges.
These will wear down along the edges.

But this toothy thing is not yet over.
This part of growing and getting older.
Suzie was up high on the swing.
When another tooth came out flying.

"Where is my tooth?" Suzie asks.
"I've been through this in the past!".
"My new tooth will be here one day."
"Until then I will continue to play!".

CPSIA information can be obtained
at www.ICGtesting.com
Printed in the USA
JSHW061336060223
37305JS00003B/8

9 780999 138533